BRISBANE

» IN PHOTOS «

Larissa Dening

BRISBANE

» IN PHOTOS «

EXPLORE
AUSTRALIA

» INTRODUCTION

I have seen a significant change in Brisbane in the 18 years I've lived here. I've watched it grow and transform from what was once a big old country town into a laidback, vibrant city. Though I have travelled all over the world, I am always happy to come back home and enjoy the perfect weather, amazing food, friendly faces and chilled-out atmosphere.

Photographing my hometown for this project made me fall in love with Brisbane all over again, gaining a newfound appreciation for areas I knew well and ones I had all but forgotten. From the Eat Street Markets to the laneways of Fortitude Valley to ever-popular Southbank, I discovered rooftop bars, a thriving food scene, an amazing collection of street art and an eclectic mix of old sandstone buildings and sleek, modern highrises.

Brisbane is a very picturesque city – one that often gets overlooked by tourists who don't realise it's so much more than a stopover on the way to Sydney or the Great Barrier Reef. The city wraps beautifully around its winding river, dotted with striking bridges, sunny cliffs and beautiful green spaces to relax in on a hot summer's day. CityCat boats and ferries cruise along the river, basking under Brisbane's expansive sky, before dropping passengers off at hip neighbourhoods full of pretty streets and hidden treasures. And then there's what you'll find just outside the city: sun-drenched coastlines, tranquil islands and temperate rainforest hinterlands. This city's all grown up and worth exploring in its own right.

Welcome to my city!

LARISSA DENING

» **LEFT** Brisbane City comes to life as the sun rises over Southbank

» **PREVIOUS** Fishermen enjoying the last of the day's light at Shorncliffe Pier

» **ABOVE** This brick house in Newmarket holds one of Brisbane's hidden treasures: Crust & Co Artisan Bakery, home to some of the city's best baked goods

» **RIGHT** *Pride*, a statue on the corner of Charlotte and Albert streets, stands opposite the former Festival Hall, where The Beatles played in 1964

» **OPPOSITE** Beautifully restored City Hall, built in the 1920s, sits in King George Square

» **LEFT** An aerial view of Shorncliffe Pier, one of Australia's longest recreational piers

» **ABOVE** Pretty pink mornings at Southbank featuring the Wheel of Brisbane, Queensland Performing Arts Centre and the ABC Brisbane building

» **OPPOSITE** Southbank's Streets Beach is just next to the river and a popular place to cool off in summer months

» RIGHT Shrine of Remembrance in ANZAC Square between Anne and Adelaide streets

» **RIGHT** Hanging desserts inside Cowch Dessert Cocktail Bar tantalise passers-by in Southbank

» **OPPOSITE** Locals and tourists walk through Southbank's bougainvillea archway

» **OVERLEAF** City views at night from Southbank

» **ABOVE** Grab some food and a seat, then enjoy the atmosphere at Eat Street Markets, Hamilton

» **FAR LEFT** The famous Golden Gaytime Conut at Eat Street Markets, Hamilton

» **LEFT** A warm welcome to Eat Street Markets

» **OPPOSITE** Eat Street Markets' laneway of food

» **OVERLEAF** Brisbane witnesses some amazing lightning storms, particularly in the summer months

» **ABOVE** This hidden cafe, tucked down the alleyway next to Irish Murphy's in Brisbane's CBD, is a great little spot to get away from the hustle and enjoy a latte or two

» **LEFT** The beautiful gardens at Roma Street Parkland

» **OPPOSITE** Archive Fine Books, one of the largest second-hand bookstores in the world, is full of the heady scents of paper and ink

» **ABOVE** Old newspaper company sign written across a building in Queen Street Mall

» **OPPOSITE** The Myer Centre on popular Queen Street Mall is a great place to catch a movie or do a spot of shopping

» **LEFT** City Botanic Gardens is a beautiful green space tucked between the city's skyscrapers and the river, full of places to relax, ride a bike, have a picnic or play a game of cricket

» **OVERLEAF** Sunset bathes Brisbane CBD and the Brisbane River, as seen from Kangaroo Point

» **ABOVE** The stunning Treasury Casino holds a hotel, six restaurants, five bars and a nightclub

» **OPPOSITE** Wandering the majestic corridors of St John's Cathedral on Anne Street

» **ABOVE** The Wickham in Fortitude Valley is a long-time favourite watering hole for Brisbane locals

» **LEFT** Part of the heritage-listed NAB Bank was converted into seriously popular The Gresham Bar on Queen Street

» **OPPOSITE** After an extensive refurbishment and with an awesome outdoor courtyard, The Wickham is now one of Brisbane's go-to bars

» LEFT Customs House on a clear night in Brisbane

» **ABOVE** One of many cute shops and cafes in Winn Lane, Fortitude Valley

» **OPPOSITE** My favourite piece of street art in Brisbane, right beside Winn Lane in Fortitude Valley

» **ABOVE** All kinds of colourful characters, like this busker, can be found in the city

» **RIGHT** Tucked away at the bottom of Burnett Lane, Brew Cafe & Wine Bar offers refuge from the inner-city chaos

» ABOVE Old and new buildings surround Post Office Square in Brisbane's CBD

» RIGHT Flying high above Moreton Island, south-east of Brisbane, and its incredible shipwrecks just offshore

» **ABOVE** Stunningly peaceful and meticulous Japanese Garden in the Brisbane Botanic Gardens, Mt Coot-tha

» **OPPOSITE** The famous dome in the tropical gardens at the Brisbane Botanic Gardens, Mt Coot-tha

» **OVERLEAF** Kurilpa Bridge, a pedestrian footbridge connecting South Brisbane to the CBD, is particularly pretty at night

» **ABOVE** Fish Lane in hip West End is filled with stunning street art

» **RIGHT** The moon shines bright in Fish Lane, West End

» **OPPOSITE** View down a new urban sanctuary: Fish Lane in West End

» **ABOVE** Heritage-listed City Hall looking stately in King George Square

» **OPPOSITE** The stunning main auditorium inside Brisbane's City Hall

» **OVERLEAF** There are plenty of rooftop bars around Brisbane, but you can't beat the Stock Exchange Hotel on Edward Street for stunning city views

中國城

» ABOVE You can find some of the city's best Asian cuisine in Chinatown Mall, Fortitude Valley

» LEFT Statues and water fountains are scattered throughout Chinatown Mall, Fortitude Valley

» OPPOSITE Neon lights of Bakery Lane, Fortitude Valley

» ABOVE Historic MacArthur Chambers building, home to Brisbane's flagship Apple store

» **ABOVE** Cute little mural decorates a window in Fortitude Valley

» **OVERLEAF** Full moon rising over Shorncliffe Pier

» **ABOVE** Brisbane Powerhouse is a repurposed powerhouse now used as a venue for plays, concerts and other events

» **RIGHT** There's nothing like a Queensland pineapple picked up at the market

» **OPPOSITE** The Jan Powers Farmers Market at the Powerhouse in New Farm is a popular place for locals to collect regional produce on a Saturday morning

» **ABOVE** Mirrored skyscrapers reflect light from the sky over Elizabeth Street

» **OPPOSITE** American-style street art in Eagle Lane

» **OVERLEAF** Story Bridge peeking between the giant sandstone columns of Customs House

» **ABOVE** Fortitude Valley's hipster hangout, Ric's Bar: great music, beer and entertainment

» **LEFT** Lazy Sunday brunch in Bakery Lane, Fortitude Valley

» **OPPOSITE** Ash and Monties Cafe stays true to the urban landscape of West End by using local street art talent to decorate the space

» RIGHT Views over Main Beach, Point Lookout on North Stradbroke Island, a short drive from Brisbane City

» **ABOVE** Old Rialto Theatre sign still stands above what are now converted shops and restaurants in West End

» **RIGHT** Once used as a cinema, this iconic piece of architecture in West End is a lovely reminder of days gone by

» **ABOVE** Some of the city's cutest graffiti lives in Newstead

» **LEFT** The latest installation out the front of Gallery of Modern Art (GOMA), Southbank

» **OPPOSITE** Brisbane mixes old and new, like the heritage-listed Albert Street Uniting Church surrounded by a cluster of modern buildings

» **OVERLEAF** Palm trees at Southbank's Streets Beach

» **ABOVE** Nighttime swims in the pool at Next Hotel on Queen Street come with a glowing view of the Treasury Casino

» **OPPOSITE** Pop-up igloo bars at Customs House, with a view of the river and the Story Bridge

» **ABOVE** Inviting storefronts along Latrobe Terrace, Paddington

» **LEFT** Fundies Organic Market offers healthy treats in the inner-city suburb of Paddington

» **OPPOSITE** Quaint boutique shops line the streets of the funky inner-city suburb of Paddington

» **ABOVE** Along the Brisbane River at Eagle Street Pier, swanky restaurants come alive at night

» **OPPOSITE** View of the glowing city skyline and Kurilpa Bridge, as seen from Victoria Bridge

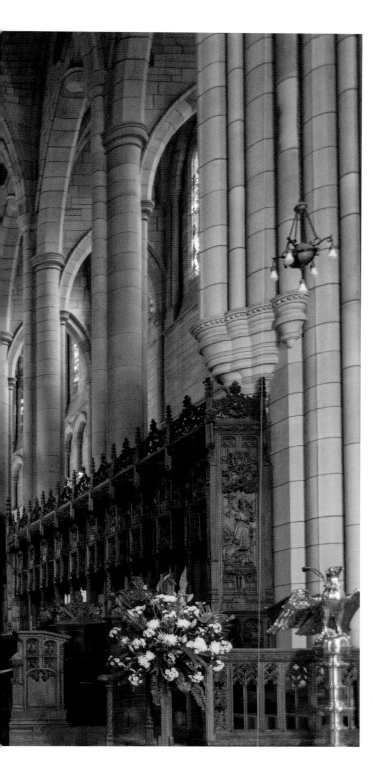

» **LEFT** St John's Cathedral is one of the most beautiful churches in Brisbane

» **ABOVE** Beautiful, iconic sandstone buildings surround a massive green space at the University of Queensland in St Lucia

» **OPPOSITE** Reflection pools like this one make the University of Queensland's St Lucia campus one of the state's most picturesque campuses

» **ABOVE** Brunch at Lost Boys Cafe, Fortitude Valley

» **ABOVE** Nepalese Peace Pagoda at Southbank, built for World Expo '88

» **OVERLEAF** Picnics at sunset from New Farm Park

» **ABOVE** Views over Frenchmans Bay, North Stradbroke Island

» **PREVIOUS** Double rainbow over historic Shorncliffe Pier

» **ABOVE** Watching out for the waves in a gorge on North Stradbroke Island

» **OVERLEAF** Brisbane Arts Theatre is an 80-year-old independent theatre company that showcases local talent in big-name productions

» **ABOVE** Heritage-listed, Victorian-style Regatta Hotel boasts 140 years of history

» **OPPOSITE** Sunday afternoon socialising at the iconic Regatta Hotel, Toowong

» RIGHT Rooftop views over Brisbane at sunset from Eleven Rooftop Bar, Fortitude Valley

» **ABOVE** Mister Fitz is on top of a new craze sweeping Brisbane: doughnuts and ice-cream

» **ABOVE** Manly Boat Harbour at sunrise

» **LEFT** Bagel street art on the side of Scout Cafe on Petrie Terrace

» **OVERLEAF** About 90 minutes west of Brisbane, you'll find endless fields of huge yellow sunflowers each summer

» ABOVE A two-storey mural of Muhammed Ali in Fish Lane, West End

» **ABOVE** Back lanes of West End are filled with uber-cool restaurants and bars

» **ABOVE** Next Rooftop Pool and Bar, suspended right in the middle of the city

» **OPPOSITE** Inside view of the beautifully restored City Hall

» **ABOVE** Views down to the river at sunset, framed by the Kangaroo Point Rotunda

» **OPPOSITE** Rock climbing is a popular sport amongst tourists and locals at Kangaroo Point Cliffs

» **OVERLEAF** Those perfect sunny days at Southbank, full of flowers and the glint of the Wheel of Brisbane

» LEFT Once a year, Brisbane holds its massive Riverfire festival, which includes an impressive fireworks display

» **ABOVE** Felix Espresso and Wine Bar in Burnett Lane is a hideaway cafe serving local and organic goodies

» **LEFT** Take a stroll down Burnett Lane, where you'll come across all sorts of street art

» **ABOVE** Elegant, heritage-listed Brisbane Arcade links Adelaide Street and Queen Street Mall

» **ABOVE** Brunching in chic cafes is the thing to do in James Street, Fortitude Valley

» **FAR LEFT** Fashionable James Street in Fortitude Valley is lined with designer shops and expensive cars

» **LEFT** Fish Lane is full of interesting pieces of street art

» **OPPOSITE** The colourful, street art-filled Burnett Lane, Brisbane City

» **OVERLEAF** Story Bridge is a twinkling nighttime fixture

» **ABOVE** Amazing restaurants meet chic street art in Fish Lane, West End

» **RIGHT** River and Story Bridge views from the historic Customs House

» **OPPOSITE** Modern lines and sculptures frame the vintage beauty of City Hall's clock tower

»ABOVE Inside the stunningly beautiful Regents Theatre in Queen Street Mall

»OPPOSITE With an aesthetic inspired by the glitzy glamour of South Beach in Miami, Sandy's Good Time Bar in Paddington is the place to have fun

» RIGHT Sunset views from Kangaroo Point Cliffs are unparalleled

» **LEFT** Street art meets skyscrapers on Elizabeth Street

»ABOVE Winding pathways in Roma Street Parklands

» **ABOVE** Parks Alive Festival, Roma Street Parklands

» **LEFT** Inner-city lake and tranquil green space in Roma Street Parklands

» **OVERLEAF** North Stradbroke Island offers endless beaches that double as roadways

» ABOVE Sunset views and picnics at Mt Coot-tha

»ABOVE Shoppers going about their business in Queen Street Mall

» **ABOVE** Views of the old woolstores-turned-chic apartments of Newstead, as seen from the CityCat ferry

» ABOVE Fresh-brewed ale is always on offer at Green Beacon Brewing Co in Newstead

» **ABOVE** Couple enjoys one of the walkways that winds alongside the Brisbane River

» **OPPOSITE** Mountain goat street art on the side of Scout Cafe, Petrie Terrace

» **ABOVE** The stunningly picturesque Elabana Falls, a 1.5-hour drive south of Brisbane in the rainforest hinterland of Lamington National Park

» **OPPOSITE** Lone Pine Koala Sanctuary, only 15 minutes west of the CBD, is filled with cute animals you can cuddle

» RIGHT Nighttime views over the river from Kangaroo Point Cliffs

» **ABOVE** Ornate old windows sit above modern shops along Queen Street Mall

» **OPPOSITE** Beautiful butterfly facade above Zara in Queen Street Mall

» ABOVE Colourful facade of Sangria Bar, Southbank

Many years from now, a girl was born into an endless city.

» **ABOVE** There is a lot to discover in Winn Lane, Fortitude Valley

» **OVERLEAF** Daytime views over Brisbane from Sofitel Hotel

» ABOVE City Botanic Gardens is a great place to take a break from the hustle of the CBD

» **ABOVE** Visits to Brisbane would be incomplete without a ride up and down the Brisbane River on the CityCat ferry

» **OVERLEAF** Bougainvillea and sunset clouds frame the Story Bridge

Published in 2018 by Hardie Grant Travel, a division of
Hardie Grant Publishing

Hardie Grant Travel (Melbourne)
Building 1, 658 Church Street
Richmond, Victoria 3121

Hardie Grant Travel (Sydney)
Level 7, 45 Jones Street
Ultimo, NSW 2007

hardiegranttravel.com

Explore Australia is an imprint of Hardie Grant Travel

A Cataloguing-in-Publication entry is available from
the catalogue of the National Library of Australia at
www.nla.gov.au

Brisbane in Photos
ISBN 9781741175585

Commissioning editor
Melissa Kayser

Project editor
Kate J. Armstrong

Editorial assistant
Aimee Barrett

Design
Erika Budiman

Typesetting
Megan Ellis

Prepress
Megan Ellis and Splitting Image Colour Studio

Printed in China by 1010 Printing International Limited

» **COVER AT TOP & BACK COVER** Some of the city's cutest graffiti lives
in Newstead

» **COVER AT BOTTOM** Nothing beats autumn sunsets over the city,
the river and the Story Bridge, seen from Wilsons Outlook in
New Farm